REMARKABLE CANADIANS

Roberta Bondar

by Leia Tait

Published by Weigl Educational Publishers Limited
6325 10 Street SE
Calgary, Alberta, Canada
T2H 2Z9

Website: www.weigl.com
Copyright ©2009 Weigl Educational Publishers Limited

All of the Internet URLs given in the book were valid at the time of publication.
However, due to the dynamic nature of the Internet, some addresses may have changed,
or sites may have ceased to exist since publication. While the author and publisher
regret any inconvenience this may cause readers, no responsibility for any such changes
can be accepted by either the author or the publisher.

Library and Archives Canada Cataloguing in Publication data available upon request.
Fax (403) 233-7769 for the attention of the Publishing Records department.

ISBN 978-1-55388-482-8 (hard cover)
ISBN 978-1-55388-483-5 (soft cover)

Printed in the United States of America
1 2 3 4 5 6 7 8 9 0 12 11 10 09 08

Editor: Heather C. Hudak
Design: Terry Paulhus

Photograph Credits
Canadian Space Agency: pages 5 front, 9; Getty Images: pages 1, 3, 5 back, 7 top,
7 top middle, 7 top right, 7 bottom left, 13 top right, 13 top left, 13 middle right,
13 middle left, 13 bottom, 14, 20; McMaster University: page 8; NASA: pages 10,
12, 16; Newscom: pages 17, 18, 19.

Every reasonable effort has been made to trace ownership and to obtain
permission to reprint copyright material. The publishers would be pleased
to have any errors or omissions brought to their attention so that they may
be corrected in subsequent printings.

We gratefully acknowledge the financial support of the Government of Canada
through the Book Publishing Industry Development Program (BPIDP) for our
publishing activities.

Contents

Who Is Roberta Bondar?

"Life's a journey. Basically, we're just hanging out and seeing what we can do with what we have."

Roberta Bondar is Canada's first woman astronaut. She is a doctor, scientist, author, and photographer. Roberta has spent her life studying how people see and understand the world. She is especially interested in how their minds and bodies react to changes in their surroundings. Roberta has made important discoveries in space medicine. Her writings and photos have helped people see the world in new ways. She is truly a remarkable Canadian.

Growing Up

Roberta Bondar was born on December 4, 1945. She grew up in Sault Ste. Marie, Ontario. She lived with her parents, Edward and Mildred, and her older sister, Barbara.

As a child, Roberta was fascinated by science. She had her own laboratory equipment, including a chemistry set and a microscope. Roberta used these tools to carry out experiments in the basement of her family's home.

Roberta was especially interested in space. She read many books on the topic. Some were factual. Others were fictional, or make-believe. They told of heroic men and women who had fantastic adventures in outer space. This was also the theme of Roberta's favourite television show, *Flash Gordon*. Roberta dreamed of travelling through space like the characters in these stories. At night, she searched the sky for stars and **satellites**. During the day, she built model spaceships and tried to contact space beings on her radio.

Short films about comic book superhero Flash Gordon aired in theatres between 1936 and 1940. In the 1950s, there was also a *Flash Gordon* TV show.

Ontario Tidbits

BIRD
Common Loon

TREE
Eastern White Pine

FLOWER
White Trillium

The city of Sault Ste. Marie sits on St. Mary's River between Lake Superior and Lake Huron.

At its widest point, Ontario stretches 1,628 kilometres from east to west.

First Nations have lived in Ontario for more than 7,000 years.

About one-third of the world's fresh water is held in Ontario's lakes.

Ontario's **shield of arms** has three golden maple leaves on a green background. The shield appears on the provincial flag.

Think about it!

Ontario is home to the David Florida Laboratory. This is a world-class research centre where spacecraft are built and tested. Think about the province where you live. What space science programs are near you? Use the Internet to find space-related programs and facilities in your province. Search for terms such as astronauts, planets, space, spacecraft, and stars with the name of your province.

Practice Makes Perfect

As a teen, Roberta attended Sir James Dunn Collegiate and Vocational School in Sault Ste. Marie. She led the school's science team and won an **honourable mention** at the Canada Wide Science Fair. During the summers, she studied insects as a researcher for the Ontario Department of Fisheries and Forestry.

After finishing high school, Roberta decided to become a scientist. She spent many years earning science **degrees** from the University of Guelph, the University of Western Ontario, and the University of Toronto. In 1977, Roberta earned a medical degree from McMaster University. She specialized in space medicine and **neurology**. Part of her research focussed on how astronauts react to reduced gravity in space.

In 1983, the Canadian government created the Canadian Astronaut Program. The government wanted six people to fly in future space missions. Roberta was thrilled and applied right away. Her application was selected, and she began the steps toward becoming an astronaut.

🍁 McMaster University is located in Hamilton, Ontario.

Before she could become an astronaut, Roberta had to complete a number of tests and interviews. The process took many months. Finally, on December 3, 1983, Roberta and five others were selected to become the first Canadian astronauts. Roberta was the only woman in the group.

QUICK FACTS

- Roberta learned how to fly single-engine planes before she learned how to drive a car. She earned her pilot's license in 1968.

- As a neurologist, Roberta studied the **nervous system**, the eye, and the inner ear.

- As part of her astronaut training, Roberta learned to scuba dive and to parachute.

Roberta and the others began astronaut training in 1984. They learned how shuttle systems operate and how astronauts live in space. They researched topics in space science and designed experiments for future missions. Roberta trained for eight years before having the chance to go to space.

More than 4,300 Canadians applied to the Canadian Astronaut Program in 1983. It was a dream come true for Roberta to be chosen for the program.

Key Events

On January 22, 1992, Roberta finally achieved her dream of going to space. She lifted off onboard space shuttle *Discovery*. The *Discovery* space shuttle was the first shuttle equipped with a fully functional laboratory. The International **Microgravity** Laboratory was created by scientists from around the world. It had the tools the astronauts needed to study how living things and objects behave in space. On the mission, Roberta performed 42 experiments for more than 200 scientists from 14 countries. Many of the experiments looked for ways future astronauts could spend more time in space.

The *Discovery* mission lasted eight days. The shuttle travelled almost 5,407,000 kilometres and circled Earth 129 times. It landed at Edwards Air Force Base in California on January 30, 1992. Roberta was welcomed as a hero.

❧ The *Discovery* crew was made up of three pilot astronauts, two mission specialists, and two payload specialists.

Thoughts from Roberta

As a child, Roberta wanted to go into space. Here are some of the things she has said about her interests and her life.

Roberta is proudly Canadian.

"When you see your own country from space, it is an extraordinary experience."

Roberta experiences microgravity onboard *Discovery*.

"Suddenly there is no more **acceleration** and no more pressure on my body. It is like being at the top of a roller coaster and my whole body is in free-fall. My helmet is no longer heavy. Everything feels like it wants to float away from me, even the camera."

As a young girl, Roberta dreamed of flying.

"I always thought birds had it over me. They could fly and see Earth at great distances, and I thought they were beautiful. So it was natural for me to want to fly."

Roberta believes there is life on other planets.

"There are kajillions of billions of stars—why wouldn't there be other life forms?"

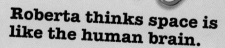

Roberta thinks space is like the human brain.

"We look at the kabillions of stars that are out there and we look at the kadrillions of **neurons** inside the brain and we still don't know how to connect all the stuff together."

Roberta believes knowledge is key to success.

"Stop and say, 'What am I looking at here?' Take the time to see where you are."

What Is an Astronaut?

An astronaut is someone who flies on a spacecraft, such as a shuttle. Canadian astronauts work for the Canadian Space Agency (CSA). The CSA manages Canada's space science and technology programs. Canadian astronauts work closely with other space agencies, such as the National Aeronautics and Space Administration (NASA) in the United States.

There are three main types of astronauts. They are pilot astronauts, mission specialists, and **payload** specialists. Pilot astronauts command shuttle missions. They fly the shuttle and make sure it works properly. Mission specialists do specific jobs during a mission. They might carry out experiments, operate equipment, launch satellites, or perform a spacewalk. Payload specialists are professional scientists. They become astronauts to perform complex scientific experiments in space. Roberta was a payload specialist on space shuttle *Discovery*.

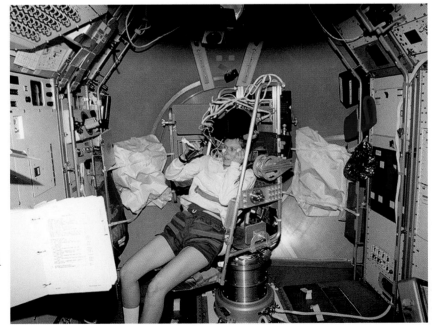

🍁 Payload specialists, such as Roberta Bondar, have specific knowledge about the purpose of the payload and know what needs to be done with it when it reaches space.

Astronauts 101

Marc Garneau (1949–)

Missions *Challenger*, 1984; *Endeavour*, 1996 and 2000
Achievements Like Roberta, Marc Garneau was one of Canada's first six astronauts. In 1984, he became the first Canadian in space. He flew as a payload specialist on space shuttle *Challenger*. Later, Marc worked for NASA's **Mission Control Center**, where he communicated with astronauts on shuttle missions. Marc was a mission specialist on space shuttle *Endeavour* in 1996 and again in 2000, when he helped build the **International Space Station** (ISS). Marc later served as president of the CSA.

Chris Hadfield (1959–)

Missions *Atlantis*, 1995; *Endeavour*, 2001
Achievements Chris Hadfield has been an astronaut since 1992. In 1995, Chris was a mission specialist on space shuttle *Atlantis*. He was the first Canadian to operate the **Canadarm** when the shuttle docked with Russian space station *Mir*. Chris is the only Canadian ever to board *Mir*. In 2001, he was a mission specialist on space shuttle *Endeavour*. On this mission, he became the first Canadian to perform a spacewalk. Today, Hadfield is chief of ISS operations.

Steve MacLean (1954–)

Missions *Columbia*, 1992; *Atlantis*, 1996
Achievements: Before becoming an astronaut, Steve MacLean was a laser scientist. From 1987 to 1993, Steve supervised the Advanced Space Vision System (ASVS). This was a computerized camera that astronauts used to guide the Canadarm in space. In 1992, Steve was a payload specialist on space shuttle *Challenger*. He was a mission specialist on space shuttle *Atlantis* in 1996. Today, Steve is the chief astronaut for the CSA.

Julie Payette (1963–)

Missions *Discovery*, 1999
Achievements Julie Payette is Canada's second woman astronaut. Like Chris Hadfield, she was one of four Canadians chosen for astronaut training in 1992. Julie is an expert in computer science. She helped create an advanced **robotics** system for the ISS. In 1999, Julie was a mission specialist on space shuttle *Discovery*. During the mission, *Discovery* docked with the ISS. Payette operated the Canadarm and became the first Canadian to board the ISS.

Space Shuttle

The space shuttle takes astronauts into space. It has three main parts. The orbiter carries the astronauts and cargo. Rocket boosters propel the orbiter into space. The fuel tank holds fuel for the engines. During launch, the orbiter accelerates at 3,218 kilometres per minute. It can stay in orbit for about two weeks.

Influences

The greatest influence in Roberta's life has been her family. Her mother, father, and sister have helped Roberta become the person she is today. Without their love and support, she may not have been able to become a scientist or fly in space.

As a child, Roberta loved playing sports and studying science. During the 1950s and 1960s, some people thought these activities were only for boys. Roberta's parents encouraged her to follow her dreams. They cheered at her sports games and bought her science equipment so she could do experiments. They told Roberta to do what she loved, no matter what other people thought.

🍁 Roberta enjoys many outdoor pursuits, such as canoeing.

When Roberta was 11, her parents gave her a camera. Soon, she was taking photos of everything around her. As she grew up, Roberta often used photos in her work as a scientist. In fact, one of her special duties on space shuttle *Discovery* was photographing Earth from the shuttle windows. Roberta was awed by the beautiful view. It made her want to see more of Earth from the ground. Later, Roberta earned a degree in professional nature photography. In 2000, she published her first book of photos, called *Passionate Vision: Discovering Canada's National Parks*.

PASSIONATE VISION

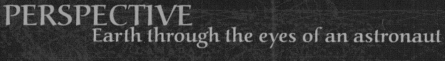

PERSPECTIVE
Earth through the eyes of an astronaut

As an astronaut, scientist and a photographer, Dr. Roberta Bondar has a consuming interest in how we look at things. From her post-doctoral work in neuro-ophthalmology – how we see and record the world around us – to her mission aboard the space shuttle Discovery as a Canadian astronaut in 1992, she has always used photography to understand natural processes. She has photographed through microscopes and portholes. On board Discovery her duties included photographing the Earth and working closely with NASA's Earth Observation team.

An accomplished landscape and nature photographer, Dr. Bondar has photographed all of Canada's 41 national parks. A book of these photographs, *Passionate Vision*, was published last year and an exhibition of the work is touring Canada through 2002. Dr. Bondar's work reflects the unique perspective of someone who has documented the earth from both the ground and from space. This site is designed to represent our planet through her dual points of view.

continue

In 1997, Roberta began photographing Canada's national parks. She was the first person to photograph all 41 of these parks. In her photos, Roberta tried to capture the special beauty of each place. She hoped to inspire people to care more for Earth. She wanted people to feel more respect and responsibility for nature. *Passionate Vision* became a best seller when it was published. Roberta's photos were also displayed by the Canadian Museum of Nature. To view a sample of her photos, visit **www.kodak.com/US/en/corp/features/bondar**.

Overcoming Obstacles

Roberta faced many obstacles in her journey to space. One of the most difficult was learning how to cope with microgravity. Weightlessness in space often causes astronauts to become sick. It also makes work difficult, because anything that is not tied down floats away. Roberta spent thousands of hours preparing for this experience.

She practised her experiments over and over to make sure she would get them right in space. She took trips on a special airplane that recreates the feeling weightlessness of space. She also spent years learning how astronauts' bodies and minds react to the stress of space travel. These preparations helped Roberta have a successful flight.

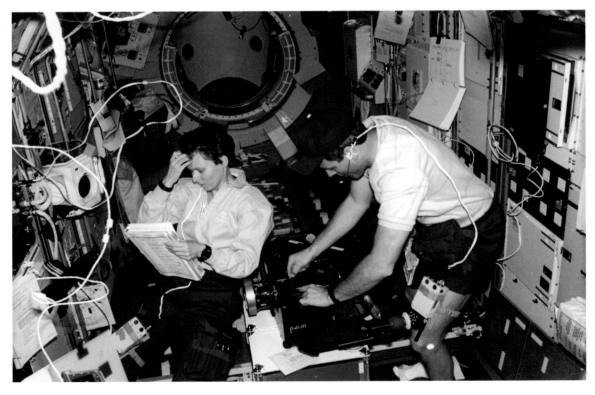

🍁 Roberta Bondar carried out experiments in a space laboratory onboard *Discovery*.

After her *Discovery* mission, Roberta continued her research. For 10 years, she led a team of researchers at NASA. They studied the effects of space travel on astronauts from 24 shuttle missions. Their findings have improved space medicine and made it easier for astronauts to cope with space travel. Roberta also has made important connections between astronauts recovering from space travel and people with neurological, or nervous system, illnesses on Earth.

Based on her experiences in space, Roberta created HyperThink™. This is a process to help people cope with change. It uses the lessons Roberta learned in space to help people face change in their daily lives. Today, Roberta travels throughout North America talking to groups about these processes. She has helped many people overcome obstacles in their lives.

🍁 Roberta retired from the CSA in 1992. She went to NASA to focus on her research with astronauts.

Achievements and Successes

Roberta has had many successes during her career. Along with *Passionate Vision*, she has written three other books. *Canada— Landscape of Dreams* and *The Arid Edge of Earth* feature more of Roberta's photos. *Touching the Earth* describes her adventures onboard space shuttle *Discovery*. Roberta also has shared her experiences as a guest on many television networks, such as BBC, CBC, CNN, Discovery, and PBS.

Roberta's accomplishments in space medicine have changed the way people think. They have inspired scientists, astronauts, and others around the world to achieve their own goals. For this reason, athletic and science awards, scholarships, gymnasiums, schools, and science centres across Canada have been named after Roberta. These things are a reminder of Roberta's energy and enthusiasm for learning. They may inspire young Canadians seeking to achieve their own dreams. Roberta has received other types of recognition as well.

🍁 Roberta enjoys meeting young people and helping them learn about science.

Following her *Discovery* mission, Roberta received the NASA Space Medal in honour of her flight. For her service to Canada, she was named an Officer of the Order of Canada in 1992. She was awarded the Commemorative Medal for the 125th Anniversary of **Confederation**. Roberta was named to the Canadian Medical Hall of Fame in 1998. The honour recognized her research in space medicine. In 2003, *Time* magazine named Roberta one of North America's best explorers.

Today, Roberta focusses on educating people about Earth and space. In 2008, she served as Canada's Honorary Patron for the International Year of Planet Earth. In that role, she raised awareness about the importance of Earth science in Canadian society.

ORDER OF CANADA

The Order of Canada is the highest honour awarded to Canadians. It recognizes those who have improved Canada and the world through their achievements. The order has three levels of membership. Companions receive the highest honours, followed by Officers, and Members. All three are given a special badge in the shape of a snowflake. The badge reads *Desiderantes meliorem patriam*, meaning "they desire a better country." More than 5,000 people have been appointed to the Order of Canada, including musicians, artists, actors, politicians, scientists, and others. To learn more about the Order of Canada, visit **www.gg.ca/honours/ nat-ord/oc/index_e.asp**.

Write a Biography

A person's life story can be the subject of a book. This kind of book is called a biography. Biographies describe the lives of remarkable people, such as those who have achieved great success or have done important things to help others. These people may be alive today, or they may have lived many years ago. Reading a biography can help you learn more about a remarkable person.

At school, you might be asked to write a biography. First, decide who you want to write about. You can choose an astronaut, such as Roberta Bondar, or any other person you find interesting. Then, find out if your library has any books about this person. Learn as much as you can about him or her. Write down the key events in this person's life. What was this person's childhood like? What has he or she accomplished? What are his or her goals? What makes this person special or unusual?

A concept web is a useful research tool. Read the questions in the following concept web. Answer the questions in your notebook. Your answers will help you write your biography review.

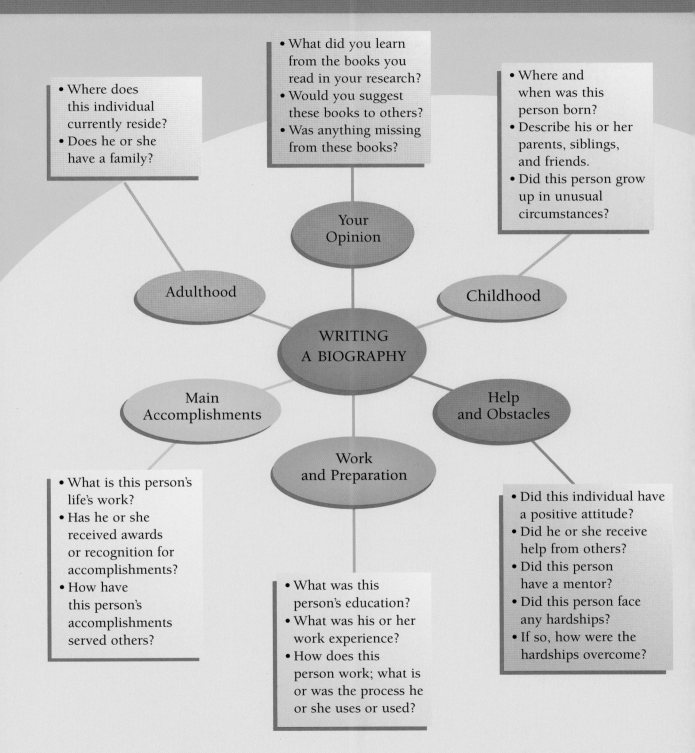

- Where does
this individual
currently reside?
- Does he or she
have a family?

- What did you learn
from the books you
read in your research?
- Would you suggest
these books to others?
- Was anything missing
from these books?

- Where and
when was this
person born?
- Describe his or her
parents, siblings,
and friends.
- Did this person grow
up in unusual
circumstances?

Your
Opinion

Adulthood

Childhood

WRITING
A BIOGRAPHY

Main
Accomplishments

Help
and Obstacles

Work
and Preparation

- What is this person's
life's work?
- Has he or she
received awards
or recognition for
accomplishments?
- How have
this person's
accomplishments
served others?

- What was this
person's education?
- What was his or her
work experience?
- How does this
person work; what is
or was the process he
or she uses or used?

- Did this individual have
a positive attitude?
- Did he or she receive
help from others?
- Did this person
have a mentor?
- Did this person face
any hardships?
- If so, how were the
hardships overcome?

Timeline

YEAR	ROBERTA BONDAR	WORLD EVENTS
1945	Roberta is born in Sault Ste. Marie, Ontario.	World War II ends.
1968	Roberta earns her first degree and her pilot's license.	Apollo 8 is the first spacecraft to orbit the Moon with humans onboard.
1977	Roberta earns a medical degree from McMaster University.	*Enterprise*, the first space shuttle orbiter, makes its first test flights over the Mojave Desert on a Boeing 747 airplane.
1983	Roberta is chosen to become one of Canada's first six astronauts.	Sally Ride becomes the first American woman in space.
1992	Roberta spends eight days in space onboard space shuttle *Discovery*.	1992 is declared the International Year of Space.
2000	Roberta publishes *Passionate Vision: Discovering Canada's National Parks*.	The first solar panels are installed on the International Space Station (ISS).
2008	Roberta is named Canada's Honorary Patron for the International Year of Planet Earth.	NASA celebrates its 50th anniversary on October 1.

Further Research

How can I find out more about Roberta Bondar?

Most libraries have computers that connect to a database that contains information on books and articles about different subjects. You can input a key word and find material on the person, place, or thing you want to learn more about. The computer will provide you with a list of books in the library that contain information on the subject you searched for. Non-fiction books are arranged numerically, using their call number. Fiction books are organized alphabetically by the author's last name.

Websites

To learn more about Roberta Bondar, visit
www.robertabondar.com

To find information about Canada's space programs and astronauts, go to www.space.gc.ca/asc/eng/default.asp

Words to Know

acceleration: increasing speed

Canadarm: a mechanical arm on the outside of a space shuttle which astronauts use to handle objects in space; designed by Canadians

Confederation: the formation of Canada on July 1, 1867

degrees: titles given to students upon completion of their studies

First Nations: members of Canada's Aboriginal community who are not Inuit or Métis

honourable mention: recognition for work or part in a competition was noteworthy, but not award-winning

International Space Station (ISS): an advanced laboratory in space being built by astronauts from 15 different countries

microgravity: the weightless environment that astronauts experience in space

Mission Control Center: the team of people who manage space missions from the ground

nervous system: the network of cells, tissues, and organs that control body responses, especially the nerves, spinal cord, and brain

neurology: the scientific study of the nervous system

neurons: cells specialized to carry information from one part of the brain to another

payload: the purpose behind a mission, or what "pays" for the flight

robotics: the science of designing and using robots for various tasks

satellites: human-made objects that are sent into orbit around a planet to gather information

shield of arms: a symbolic design representing specific aspects of heritage, used to decorate official documents and objects

Index